THE CRAFT OF
WRITING TV COMEDY

Other Allison & Busby "Writer's Guides"

THE CRAFT OF WRITING TV COMEDY

Lew Schwarz

Allison & Busby
Published by W. H. Allen & Co Plc

An Allison & Busby book
Published in 1989 by
W. H. Allen & Co Plc
Sekforde House
175/9 St John Street, London EC1V 4LL

Set in Times New Roman by Input Typesetting Ltd

Printed and bound in Great Britain by
Cox & Wyman Ltd, Reading Berkshire

ISBN 0 85031 962 5

Contents

INTRODUCTION

Genius is one per cent inspiration and
ninety-nine per cent perspiration.
Thomas Alva Edison

Television comedy writing is ninety-nine
per cent perspiration and one per cent sweat.
W. C. Black

Most people, when they watch sport on television, are content to gaze in awe at the skill, the expertise, the artistry of the games' great players. Occasionally, after a particular display of genius – a Maradonna goal, a Navratilova smash, a Steve Davis pot – they might wish they could do that, but know, deep inside, that it will never be.

When they watch comedy, however, there is hardly a living room in the country, indeed in the world, that has not heard the cry, "I could write better rubbish than that!"

Most of the criers really believe it.

Why do so few set out to prove it?

And of the comparative few who do, why do so many fail?

The obvious answer is that it is not as easy as it looks.

I have been writing comedy for television for more than 30 years. It is still not as easy as it looks.

It is a craft, as wood carving and pottery are crafts. Talent is essential, but without an understanding of the materials and a mastery of the tools, success will tend to remain elusive.

It is towards that understanding and mastery that this book hopes to lead you.

Chapter One

YOU HAD TO BE THERE

Laugh and the world laughs with you
Weep and you weep alone;
For sad old earth must borrow its mirth
But has troubles enough of its own.

Ella Wheeler Wilcox.

What is comedy?

That is one of those questions like "What is time?" – you know the answer until somebody asks you to define it.

So let us see if we can concoct a short and simple definition which will have the academics and pedants frothing at the mouth but which will suit the purpose of this book.

Comedy is the art of making people laugh.

"Well, of course! Everybody knows that," says the Parlour Pundit. "I do it all the time. I mean, well, take last Sunday down at our local. Me and Harry and Nigel, it was Harry's shout, see – three pints of lager – no, hang on – Harry was on half-pints by then – bit of waterworks trouble – he hasn't been the same since that package holiday in Lanzarote – I told him he should sue, but he won't listen, obstinate old twit – well anyway, there we were, the three of us – no, wait a minute – Nigel had popped through to the saloon to chat up the new barmaid – a right cracker, she is – I think her husband's on the oil rigs – so, anyway, Harry and me are standing there, minding our own business, when this bloke walks in – little fellow he was – came up to about here on me – and he had this enormous dog with him – like one of them Great Danes, only bigger – and up they come to the bar, right beside us, about as close as you are to me now, and the little bloke says to the barman, "A pint of bitter for me and a tomato juice for the dog." Well! I just couldn't resist it, could I. I looked straight at him – well, straight down at him and said. "Blimey! He's a big 'un!" Well! The whole place was in stitches. Everybody just fell about. Yeah, well, it might not sound funny to you now, but you should have been there."

Now, that incident in the local may indeed have been the funniest thing in the history of the world since God created Adam – (now that was really hilarious but you had to be there) – so why does the Parlour Pundit's tale have about as much comic impact as a writ?

Let us assume that the incident which PP was attempting to describe did indeed have some element of humour, which, had we been present, would temporarily have affected our equilibrium and caused us to precipitate ourselves on to the floor. Why, when PP tells it now, is the room not carpeted with wall-to-wall people?

Exactly. He told it so badly.

To tell a funny story successfully the first thing you have to come to terms with is that your listener was not there, so his absence is no excuse if your tale collapses. You must therefore give him all the relevant details which will allow him to create in his own mind the exact scene which you yourself found so mirth-provoking.

So let us look at PP's story again.

Detail he has given us in plenty, but is any of it relevant?

Does it matter to the story that it was Harry's shout? That it was three pints of lager – no, hang on, two and a half? That Harry had picked up a bug in Lanzarote, that he is an obstinate old twit? That Nigel was chatting up the barmaid whose husband might be on the oil-rigs?

Ah! At last we come to a relevant sentence. A little man walks in with a very large dog. He orders a pint of bitter for himself and a tomato juice for his animal. And the narrator looks straight at him – well, straight down at him – and says; "Blimey! He's a big 'un!"

There still seems to be something lacking. I have analyzed the information provided, relevant and other-wise, to see if there is a clue, however tenuous, that would turn "Blimey! He's a big 'un!" into a volcano of hilarity. I have not found it.

I have also tried, from over 30 years of experience, to think of some little phrase or idea, which, if inserted into the text in the right place might at least give the tag-line a smile value. I have not succeeded.

The only conclusion I can come to is that, lost and confused by his unnecessary asides, the narrator had forgotten the point of his story, if indeed he ever had one.

This phenomenon is known as borer's droop, and can be observed in all levels of society, from vicarage tea-parties to yuppie drinky-times.

To avoid this affliction all that is necessary is that, before you launch your story on what you hope will be a sea of laughter, you ask yourself three questions. Is what you are about to say essential to the plot? Does it help your audience to understand the characters and/

or the situation? Is it funny? It is also useful if you can remember the punchline.

The same three questions apply to preparing your story for television, with one great advantage. Instead of your words disappearing into X pairs of ears where, likely as not they will conjure up Y different images, they spread themselves first on paper, to be perused by a (hopefully) intelligent producer, who will pass them on to a (hopefully) competent director, who will translate them via a (hopefully) brilliant cast, into one set of pictures to be seen and (hopefully) appreciated by (hopefully) millions of viewers.

The first obstacle we have to surmount, then, is the intelligent producer.

Chapter Two

LOOK, LISTEN, LEARN

That's what I want – ready wit.
Sir Francis Cowley Burnand

Sir Francis Cowley Burnand was editor of Punch in the 1890s, the Victorian equivalent of today's light entertainment producer. His dictum, as quoted above, is still the battle-cry of those in charge of television comedy at present.

The pressures of the industry are so great that producers seldom have the time to recognize, let alone nurture, the glimmering sparks of emerging talent that float across their desks. Gone are the pioneer days of the late 50s and early 60s when you could occasionally hear a benevolent producer calling to his comical side-kick the script editor; "I say, this chap's got something! Let's have him up to town at our expense and see if we can nurture him!"

One of the more pleasant memories of my years in television took place in 1968 when I was script editor of "The Dora Bryan Show". We received a script, handwritten on four pages torn from a school jotter. The producer opened the envelope, took one look, and shot it towards the out-tray. I retrieved it. The handwriting was no worse than my own. I read it, liked it, and finally talked the producer into buying it. Some weeks later we got a second contribution from the same source. This time it was neatly typed on proper paper, a sound investment of the writer's first pay cheque As it happened, the second contribution was turned down, but at least it, and all that young writer's subsequent efforts, were given the consideration they deserved.

How then do we deal with this busy man, the producer?

We have to deal with him as we would any busy man. We have to convince him that we are not wasting his time. That we have something he not only wants but needs. There is no point in trying to sell double-glazing to a man who lives in a tent. Similarly, you don't send a long sketch, however hilarious, to a producer of a programme which uses nothing over two minutes.

What we must do is study the market; assess the performers and their styles; choose our targets; tailor our output to their needs; then, and only then, do we stand a reasonable chance of knocking on the right doors and hearing the magic word "Enter!"

To do this we need a simple piece of equipment; a television set. No television comedy writer should be without one. And when you have your television set, watch it.

Watch it at every opportunity. Regardless of your television comedy writing ambitions, watch everything.

Watch drama. Bad TV drama is a constant source of unconsciously comic ideas. Good drama will increase your knowledge and experience of sound plot construction, character relationships, and good dialogue.

Watch commercials. Since the moment the first commercials hit the screen they have provided a deep rich vein of comedy material, whether they meant to or not. Watch them avidly.

Watch documentaries. Watch nature programmes. Watch Open University and schools' programmes.

Watch them, not merely for their educational content, (which will not do you any harm in itself) but also for visual effects, for screen techniques, clear and lucid presentation, and, equally important, the seeds of comedy.

Whether your eventual aim is to emulate or indeed improve on the accomplishment and comic artistry of the Alans Bennett and Ayckbourn, or to explore the modern comedy of the human condition like Carla Lane, or even to subject the TV-watching millions to short sharp shocks of devastating wit, you must first map out the territory.

Television comedy comes in many shapes and colours. Each individual type will be discussed in the following chapters.

Study them all.

Take notes; not to plagiarise, but to learn.

Start with the comedy sketch programmes. If you see a comedy sketch which doesn't make you laugh, ask yourself why not?

As an exercise re-write it.

Study your re-write.

Is it any better?

Be honest.

Chapter Three

BREVITY IS THE WHOLE OF WIT

Laughter is the natural function of man.

Rabelais

In terms of time involved and physical energy expended the simplest form of television comedy is the quickie, or blackout sketch.

I am not saying it is easy, and it may not be your ultimate aim, but for the budding TV comedy writer the quickie has a lot going for it.

First of all, it is an exercise in brevity. (See *Hamlet*, 2, ii.).

Secondly, it is excellent practice in translating a funny idea onto paper.

Thirdly, it is the quickest way to get your name known to producers of light entertainment.

So what is a quickie or blackout sketch?

It is a sketch which will run for anything up to a minute. I have always thought of it as an animated newspaper cartoon, presented in a form which can be translated to the TV screen.

Bear in mind that TV is a visual medium, and think visually. The purest form is the one which needs no words.

Example:

EXT. TALL TOWER WITH LIGHTED
WINDOW NEAR TOP. NIGHT.
MIX TO:
INT: TOWER ROOM. NIGHT.
DAMSEL, suitably costumed, obviously in
distress, pacing the floor, gnawing knuckles,
clutching brow, etc.
CUT TO:
EXT. BUSHES AT FOOT OF TOWER.
NIGHT.
HERO, knight in armour, gazes up at window,
evinces grim determination, heroic resolve.
Starts to climb ivy-covered wall.
CUT TO:
TOWER ROOM.
DAMSEL, in deepest dejection, sobs at table.
F/X: rapping at window.
DAMSEL looks up.
Sees head and shoulders of HERO outside
window.
Cry of joy.
Dashes to window and opens it. Outwards.
Disappearance of HERO, fading yell. Distant
crash of ironmongery.
BLACKOUT.

(NOTE: keep your descriptions of action and
mood short and concise. This technique allows
a clear picture to build up in the reader.s mind.)

The next form we want to look at is one which uses
the minimum of words. Ideally the punch-line should
suffice, but on most occasions a short feed-line is
necessary, as in the following.

EXT. ESTABLISHING SHOT. HARRODS.
DAY.
MIX TO:
INT. COMPLAINTS DEPARTMENT. DAY.
This is a small counter in an opening in a wall.
A VERY SUPERIOR PERSON is standing
behind the counter, perusing a list.
CUSTOMER enters. There is a large snake
draped over his body and twined round his neck.
He does not look very happy.
The VERY SUPERIOR PERSON looks up,
regards him coldly.

                    VSP
   Sir?

                  CUSTOMER
   I was in here yesterday and bought a
mongoose. . . .
FADE.

There is another form which is simply your ordinary
common-or-garden joke set up for translation to the
screen, as:

INT. PUB. NIGHT
Two MEN sitting at table, with drinks.

                  FIRST MAN
   Did you hear about that bloke who's invented
a motor car engine that can do 180 miles to the
gallon?

                 SECOND MAN
   Yeah. It'll never catch on.

                  FIRST MAN
   Why ever not?

18

SECOND MAN

It'd take too long to save up for a cut-glass
tumbler.
FADE.

This is clearly the easiest type of quickie to write.
Strictly speaking it is not really television. It could be
done just as effectively on radio, or even on the joke
page of a local newspaper. However, it is much sought
after by Producers of sketch programmes because of
its simplicity and because it can be accommodated in
any setting that is available. The two Ronnies, for
instance, could do this piece in the pub as written, as
the two old men lounging on their allotment, as the two
tramps sitting in the field, or even in their characters of
the two village idiots.

An extension of the quickie form is the running gag.
This consists of variations on a theme and is highly
attractive to sketch-show producers because it enables
them to use the same set over and over again and thus
save money.

Take, for instance the situation of a conjurer and his
vanishing cabinet. Let us see how many variations we
can get out of it.

1.
SCENE: A STAGE.
Stage Centre – A conjurer's vanishing cabinet.
ATTRACTIVE CONJURER'S ASSISTANT
(ACA) posing beside it.
F/X: Suitable Music
Enter CONJURER in full rig – white tie and
tails, cane, cape, top-hat, gloves.
Elegantly, to the accompanying music, he peels

off gloves, cape, top-hat, and hands them, with his cane, to the ACA.

The ACA exits with garments.

The CONJURER approaches the cabinet, demonstrates its emptiness and lack of concealed apartments.

The ACA returns, empty-handed.

She joins the CONJURER centre-stage. He mimes his intention of placing her in the cabinet. She reacts with appropriate gestures.

The CONJURER places her in the cabinet, closes the door.

He makes his magic passes.

There is a flash of light and puff of smoke from in front of the cabinet.

It clears.

The cabinet has disappeared, leaving a rather perplexed girl behind.

And a bewildered CONJURER in front.
FADE.

2.
SCENE: A STAGE.
Setting as in 1.

Repeat opening business exactly as in 1, up to CONJURER's mime of intention.

Still trying to maintain his suavity, the CONJURER leads the assistant to the cabinet.

He leaves her for a moment to have quick, rather nervous, last check of the interior. It seems all right.

He resumes his poise, bows her in, closes door.

He makes his magic passes.

Flash and smoke.

It clears.

The CONJURER takes a quick glance. The cabinet is reassuringly there.

Triumphantly he throws the door open. The ACA is inside, completely naked, trying desperately to hide the important bits behind her hands.

The CONJURER hurriedly closes the door and puts his back against it, trying to force a smile.
FADE.

3.
SCENE: A STAGE.
Setting as in 1.

Repeat opening business as in 1, but with CONJURER showing grim determination to get it right this time.

When he has divested himself of his outer garments and sent them off with ACA he turns and strides resolutely up to the cabinet.

He pulls the door open.

And finds himself looking straight at an oncoming train.

He slams the door shut and braces himself against it.
FADE.

4.
SCENE: A STAGE.
Setting as in 1.

Repeat opening business as in 1, but this time the CONJURER's nerves are beginning to show. His examination and display of the emptiness of the cabinet is much more intense. Eventually he is satisfied.

The ACA joins him on stage.

He mimes his intention of putting her in the cabinet.

Still nervous he decides to check again.
He goes to the cabinet, throws the door wide open. It is clearly empty. He smiles, relieved.

He returns to the girl, confidently repeats the mime of his intention.

They both turn towards the cabinet.

The door opens a few inches. A hand comes out holding a couple of empty milk bottles, which it deposits on the floor. The cabinet door closes.

The CONJURER and the girl freeze, staring openmouthed at the phenomenon.

A MILKMAN enters, picks up the empties, puts down a fresh bottle and exits.

The hand comes out again, takes the fresh bottle in. The door closes.

The CONJURER dashes forward, opens the door. The cabinet is empty.
FADE.

5.
SCENE: A STAGE.
Setting as in 1.

Repeat opening business as in 1, CONJURER and girl now beginning to look hollow-eyed and haunted.

They reach the mime of intention.

Before they can start to move towards the cabinet there is the sound of approaching footsteps.

They look towards the cabinet.

The footsteps get louder. They stop. The

cabinet door opens apparently of its own accord. It closes. There is a pause of as long as the director can allow.

There is the sound of a toilet flushing.

The door opens, closes. The footsteps die away.

The CONJURER and girl look at each other, shrug helplessly.

FADE.

This sequence illustrates what can be done with one simple basic concept.

Moral: never throw away a funny idea. Another day, another look at it, and you may find you have another quickie.

Take the situation which we discussed in Chapter one – the pub/little man/big dog/brash customer situation. As an exercise, see how many quickie variations you can come up with. Take the pub as a constant, and vary the other ingredients.

Give the big dog to the brash customer and see if that will suggest a useful twist.

Try big man/little dog.

Make one of the characters a woman, large/bossy, perhaps, or Sloane Ranger type.

Try a different pet; gerbil, parrot, a talking aspidistra.

Keep asking yourself, "What if. . . ?"

You may not come up with an immediate winner, but you will have some fun.

Chapter Four

THERE WERE THESE TWO FELLAHS. . . .

His eye begets occasion for his wit
For every object that the one doth catch
The other turns to a mirth-moving jest.
Love's Labour's Lost.

Most light entertainment shows nowadays are composed of quickies and short sketches.

Television buffs may tell you that this is directly attributable to a very popular American show of the sixties, "Laugh-In", which pioneered the comic kaleidoscope form. Some two years before "Laugh-In" Charlie Drake had a show on ATV in which 126 sketches were crammed into six half-hours. It was just a little ahead of its time.

If the quickie is a moving newspaper cartoon the short sketch is a dramatized anecdote, usually running up to about three minutes. This is not long and no time can be wasted. The scene must be set and the characters established in the first half-dozen lines.

We are helped in this by the medium itself. Use it. The right picture at the opening of a sketch can save a lot of dialogue explanation.

Again, the purest form of this sketch is the totally visual. It is difficult to sustain for one to three minutes' time but not impossible, and a lot of course depends on the performer.

The areas in which the material for this kind of sketch can best be found are those situations where man is in conflict with machinery, or an inanimate object which does not perform as expected.

The great classic example of this form in my view is the determined golfer sketch by the late Marty Feldman, in which he pursued his golfball through every combination of impossible lies, from the back of a sand lorry, through drainpipes, to the top of a railway carriage, etc. That is the height of visual comedy to which you ought to aspire. If you don't make it first time, keep trying.

Let us take an inanimate object, say, a shooting-stick, and see if we can get a purely visual sketch out of it.

There have been sketches about shooting-sticks before, the pay-off always being the shooting-stick going off with a bang. Ours will no doubt do the same, but perhaps we can find a new way of doing it.

Supposing we set our scene in an up-market gents outfitters.

INT. UPMARKET GENTS OUTFITTERS.
Prominent sign saying: "EVERYTHING FOR THE COUNTY GENTLEMAN".
Goods on view bear this out; hatstands with tweed caps and deerstalkers; mannequins with all-weather clothing; and, to be revealed later, a display of shooting-sticks.
CUSTOMER enters, browsing. He is clearly not the type of CUSTOMER who would be expected to favour this kind of establishment. He gazes round, mildly curious.

25

He crosses to a pair of wading trousers, displayed
on the lower half of a dummy.
He circles it, finishing up at the front.
He searches and closely examines the front for
fly buttons or a zip. Finding none he shakes his
head disapprovingly and tut-tuts.
He moves on to the hat display, and tries on a
couple.
He finally selects a deerstalker, puts it on
sideways, admires himself in a nearby mirror.
Hand in jacket à la Napoleon. Has a good giggle.
Deerstalker still on head he moves on and comes
to the display of shooting-sticks.
A large sign announces: "The ULTIMO" – "The
Last Word in Shooting-Sticks!"
He examines the display with interest.
He takes one down and examines it more closely.
He hefts it.
He starts to pretend it is a rifle. Goes through a
little sequence of rifle drill, slopes arms, orders
arms, etc. with a little marching up and down.
He aims it in various directions, pretends to fire
it. Peers down the spike end. Shakes his head
in amused wonder.
He spies a placard. On it is an illustration of a
country gentleman about to place his bottom on
the saddle part of the stick.
The CUSTOMER evinces comprehension.
He opens the handles out, studies this
arrangement, realizes what it is for.
He places spike on ground, turns and sits.
There is a loud bang.
CLOSE-UP.
Head and shoulders of CUSTOMER.
Startled expression on face.

Frayed hole in top of deerstalker with wisp of
smoke coming from it.
FADE.

It is essential, when you are describing a sequence of
action or business, that you make it absolutely clear
what you want your character or characters to do. In
the film industry they have a device known as the story-
board. For an important sequence the director will
have an artist draw for him a series of pictures showing
the development of the action.

What you must try to do is to present your producer
with a story-board in words. Keep your sentences as
short as possible. Each one should describe one action.
Thus, as the producer reads, he will be seeing in his
own mind a series of clear, unambiguous pictures,
which, as they unfold, will convince him that this will
look just as funny on the screen.

In dialogue sketches you might expect the laughs to
come from the snappy lines and brilliant repartee.

So they should, but if they are the only source of
the comedy you might just as well have written a radio
sketch.

You are writing for television. Use it. Look for
action and business; action that will highlight the
dialogue; business that will bring laughs.

One of the main ingredients of drama is conflict, the
coming together of opposing views or interests. This is
doubly true of comedy. Without conflict there is very
little chance of fun. After all, it would be a very dull
tennis match if both players were on the same side of
the net.

So, one method of setting about writing a sketch is
to start off with a conflict situation.

Take a continually topical conflict situation –
smoking versus non-smoking.

We need a scene of the action.

Let us keep it simple.

We are looking for a setting where a conflict of
smoking/non-smoking interests could naturally occur.
What better place than a non-smoking compartment
on a train.

    FADE IN:
    INT. RAILWAY CARRIAGE. NON-
    SMOKER. DAY.

Right. We have our scene. Now we need characters,
and between our characters we will need contrast. We
will have a non-smoker and a smoker. The non-smoker
will be quiet and passive, the smoker loud and brash.

So let's see if we can get our characters on to the
screen and their traits established in the opening few
seconds.

    FADE IN:
    INT. RAILWAY CARRIAGE. NON-
    SMOKER. DAY.
    A quiet, respectable-looking man in pinstripes
    and a BOWLER hat is sitting in a corner reading
    his newspaper. The train is standing at a station.
    Sound F/X: Guard's whistle – train starting to
    move.
    Confused shouting – carriage door opening –
    slamming shut.
    Train gathers speed.
    Along the corridor comes a large man in
    SPORTY tweeds, cheerful and ebullient,
    carrying a copy of the *Sporting Times*.

Our characters are now in view, and their roles are clearly defined. Now we open with the first skirmish.

SPORTY comes into the compartment. With the whole compartment to choose from he flops down beside BOWLER.

SPORTY: Cor! That was a close one!

BOWLER ignores him and goes on reading, retreating even further behind his paper. SPORTY reaches over, grabs BOWLER's wrist forcing him to lower the paper.

SPORTY: I said, that was a close one.

BOWLER tries to freeze him with a look, and retires behind his newspaper. SPORTY fails to recognize the rebuff. He leans back on his seat and giggles reminiscently.

SPORTY: They tried to stop me, you know.

No response from BOWLER. SPORTY nudges him in the ribs.

SPORTY: I said, they tried to stop me. At the barrier. A little fellow. Half the size of nothing. Tried to stop me. At the barrier. I've got to catch that train, I says. It's a matter of life and death, I says. A matter of life and death? he says. Yes, I says. If I don't get away from the wife I'll kill her.

He roars with laughter, nudges BOWLER painfully in the ribs.

SPORTY: Good, that, eh? Don't get away from the wife I'll kill her.

BOWLER glares and returns to his paper.

SPORTY: Yes. I thought you'd like it. He didn't see it, though. The little fellow.

He looks across, sees that BOWLER isn't paying attention, reaches over and pulls the paper down.

SPORTY: The little fellow. You know, at the barrier. No sense of humour. Stood there. Right in front of me. "In the interests of public safety", he says, "this barrier will be shut" he went on, "one minute prior to the departure of the train" he concluded. Well, I'm a reasonable man. If that's the way you want it, I says. "That's the way I want it," he says. So I kicked him in the clippers and ran for it.

He roars with laughter. BOWLER jerks himself free, rises, moves to the diagonally opposite corner of the compartment and retires again behind his paper. SPORTY leans back, chuckling at the memory.

SPORTY: I bet it's a long time before he punches another ticket.

You will have noticed that so far in this sketch we have not yet touched on the smoker versus non-smoker theme, apart from setting the action in a non-smoking compartment. What we have managed to do, however, is to establish very firmly the two protagonists and their attitudes to each other. I find that this often happens when I start to write a sketch. It helps me to get a clear picture in my mind of how the characters will act and inter-react, and sets the parameters for the rest of the action. It will also help the producer to form a more complete picture. It may eventually be cut in the interests of time, but if it is funny it will stay in. Remember, you will be paid for the length of time your sketch appears on the screen, but there's not much chance of it staying on the screen unless it is funny.

Right. Our scene is set, our characters are introduced. Now we can get on with the main theme of our sketch, the smoker/non-smoker controversy.

> SPORTY reaches into his pockets and takes out a packet of cigarettes and a lighter. He puts a cigarette in his mouth and sparks the lighter. It does not work.
> He moves along the seat until he is sitting opposite BOWLER and taps him on the knee.

> SPORTY: Here! You gotta match?
> BOWLER: (icily) This is a non-smoker.
> SPORTY: (indignantly) Who's smoking?
> BOWLER: You are.
> SPORTY: No, I'm not. I haven't got a bleedin' light, have I?

> BOWLER looks nonplussed.

> SPORTY: Got you there, eh?

Be sparing with your directorial adverbs as in (icily)

and (indignantly) above. Use them only when you want to establish a particular mood. Certain actors and directors take such guidance as a studied insult and critical comment on their ability to interpret a role for themselves.

Sometimes they are justified.

To continue.

BOWLER retires behind his newspaper. After a moment SPORTY leans over and taps him on the knee again.

SPORTY: Well?
BOWLER: Well what?
SPORTY: Well, have you got a match or haven't you?
BOWLER: As a matter of fact, I have got a match. A whole box of them. Right here in my pocket. And that is where they are going to stay. Do you understand?
SPORTY: Yes. I understand. You're a sadist.
BOWLER: I am not a sadist. This is a non-smoking compartment. I am merely insisting on my rights.
SPORTY: Oh. Rights, is it? Justice? Fair do's? What's good enough for me is good enough for you. That sort of thing?
BOWLER: Exactly.
SPORTY: I couldn't agree more. Have a fag.

He offers the packet.

BOWLER: I do not smoke.
SPORTY: now's your chance to start. Have a fag.
BOWLER: No, thank you.

32

SPORTY: Come on. You don't know what you are missing.

BOWLER: Oh, don't I. I used to smoke. 60 a day. 60 a day for 20 years.

SPORTY: So, one more won't hurt you. Have a fag.

BOWLER: Then one day I said to myself, right! That's enough! Done! Finished! And I gave it up. Just like that!

SPORTY: Just like that, eh?

BOWLER: Just like that!

SPORTY: Good for you. Have a fag.

BOWLER: (righteous) Never again. You should try, you know. There's really nothing to it.

SPORTY: Nothing to it? Well, of course there's nothing to it. I've given up smoking thousands of times. This very morning, for instance. Got out of bed, said to myself, right! That's enough. Done. Finished. And I gave it up. Just like that.

BOWLER: But you're at it again, aren't you?

He gestures towards the cigarette in SPORTY's hand.

SPORTY: Eh? Oh. Yes. Well, the coughing stopped, didn't it. But I can give it up any time I want.

BOWLER: Go on, then.

SPORTY: You what?

BOWLER: You said you can give it up any time.

SPORTY: Yeah. Sure. Nothing to it.

BOWLER: Go ahead. Throw it out of the window.

SPORTY looks down at his hands. In one he is holding a cigarette, in the other the packet.

    SPORTY: You think I can't do it.
    BOWLER: Correct.
    SPORTY: Right, then.

He throws the cigarette out of the window.

    SPORTY: There you are.
    BOWLER: And the rest of the packet.
    SPORTY: Eh? oh, of course. No sweat.

He throws the packet out, settles back.

    SPORTY: See? Nothing to it.
    BOWLER: Well done!

SPORTY produces another packet from his pocket and strips off the wrapper.

    SPORTY: Right. Let's have a fag.

He offers the pack to BOWLER, who recoils.

    BOWLER: Get that out of my sight!

SPORTY starts searching his other pockets.

    SPORTY: Or maybe you prefer tipped. I've got
    some somewhere.
    BOWLER: (beginning to fray at edges) Tipped
    or untipped – it doesn't matter.
    SPORTY: Have an untipped, then.
    BOWLER: (getting rattier) I don't smoke. I –
    DO – NOT – SMOKE.

SPORTY: All right, mate. Calm down. Calm down. Here. What you need is a fag to steady your nerves.

BOWLER goes berserk. He leaps to his feet and starts belabouring SPORTY about the head with his newspaper.

BOWLER: Can't you get it into your skull, you great hairy oaf! I do not smoke. I have no wish to smoke. I hate people who smoke. If I were Prime Minister I would make smoking a capital offence. Down with cigarettes! Non-smokers of the world unite! You have nothing to lose but your tempers! Aaaaaarghhhh!

He runs screaming out of the compartment and along the corridor. SPORTY watches him go, baffled. He leans back in his seat, bewildered.

SPORTY: Well! If that's what giving up smoking does for you, I don't think I'll bother.

He puts a fag in his mouth and tries to get his lighter to work.
FADE.

All writing starts with an idea. Comedy writing starts with a funny idea.

Modern life is full of comedy. Look for it.

You will find it in bus queues, in supermarkets, in your own street, in your home.

Get into the habit of applying the magic formula "What if. . . ?" even in the most mundane of circumstances.

You see someone cracking an egg to make a cake.

What if the egg won't break? What if it is addled? What if it is empty?

You see a man at a bus stop with an umbrella tucked under his arm, point first. The bus arrives. He steps onto it. The crook of the umbrella catches on the post of the bus stop and stays where it it. "What if . . ." he had been making himself obnoxious, edging his way to the front of the queue? Would this make the occurrence funnier?

Sitting on a bus you find yourself, (unintentionally, of course), listening in to two conversations. Two young girls are discussing their love lives, two old ladies are exchanging gossip and medical histories. "What if . . ." you knitted these two conversations together?

The material is all around you. All you have to do is sort it out and "What if" it.

There are several basic sources of motivation. One, you have an idea which is so funny you just have to write it down. Two, you see a performer on the screen and are inspired to write a piece specifically for that performer. Three, the ideal motivation, a combination of One and Two. Four, the money is good. Five, you want to be famous.

If Five is your aim, forget it. How many comedy sketch writers can you name in one minute? If you can think of ten you are a dedicated TV comedy buff, and should probably be writing a history of the genre rather than taking part in it.

If Four, there's nothing to be ashamed of. Just remember, there is good money in brain surgery, but you need a lot of hard work and expertise to capitalize on it.

Start off with motivations One, Two and Three. If you've got what it takes, Four will follow. Be prepared to settle for that.

Chapter Five

THERE WERE THESE THREE FELLAHS. . . .

An ill-timed laugh is a dangerous evil.

Menander.

The long sketch does not seem to have too many supporters at the time of going to press. The main problem would appear to be the difficulty in sustaining the incidence of laughter over the extended period. Unless the laughs come thick and fast there is a danger of the audience becoming bored.

The normal formula for the long sketch is fairly straightforward. You take a theme and fill it with as many gags on that theme as you can create, remember, or re-write.

It is a formula that Benny Hill uses to great effect from time to time.

He takes a setting like the customs shed at Heathrow, and strings together a long sequence of what are virtually quickies, both visual and verbal. There will be funny things coming out of suitcases; he can play his oriental character with all kinds of mix-ups arising out of language difficulties, especially if one of the customs officials is also having difficulty with English; there will be inspired clowning with the brilliant supporting members of his team like Henry Magee and Bob Todd. Unfortunately, the only writing credit that appears on a "Benny Hill Show" is Benny Hill, so I cannot honestly recommend it as a potential market.

Another form of the long sketch is the comic serial as developed and perfected by the two Ronnies, with their Charley Farley/Piggy Malone Chronicles, and their hilarious "Phantom Raspberry Blower of Old London Town".

I would not recommend this type of writing to the beginner in the field of TV comedy. It is not new. We dabbled with it in the early days of TV in the 1950s. We had another go at it in the 60s with the late great Dick Emery. It never quite made it for two good reasons; low budgets, and low technology.

As the talents and skills of two established and revered performers like the two Ronnies developed, producers were prepared to budget for their capabilities, and the technology had improved to make multi-scene location work more practical. It is unlikely that a new writer in this field would receive such generous consideration.

So why should we bother to study the long sketch?

For one thing, it is a valid form of TV comedy.

For another, it is an excellent exercise in handling comic material. A basic theme can be developed and redeveloped. Different layers of character can be investigated. Gags which might stand as quickies by themselves can be expanded to produce more laughs. It gives a greater insight into the construction of a scene, and a sound grounding in scene construction is vital if you are aiming for the first division of TV comedy, the sit-com series.

And thirdly, it may make a come-back as a TV art form. After all, in these days of microscopically scrutinized programme budgets, the idea of getting perhaps five or six minutes of good strong comedy into one set is quite likely to appeal to some astute producer.

So let us look at the long sketch.

There are two basic approaches; the pseudo-realistic, and the zany.

In the pseudo-realistic approach we take a real, recognizable situation and develop our comedy from the characters we create.

A simple example is visiting time at a hospital. The patient is, let us say, an elderly man, in hospital for some minor affliction, an ingrowing toe-nail, perhaps. His visitors are his daughter, Elsie, and her husband, Fred, a couple of Jeremiahs, come ostensibly to cheer him up.

We have the set and the characters. Let us put them together and see what develops.

>   EXT. ESTABLISHING SHOT OF HOSPITAL.
>   DAY.
>   MIX TO:
>   INT. CORNER OF WARD. DAY.
>   OPEN ON CLOSE-UP of DAD in bed. He is
>   sleeping.
>
>   ELSIE: (voice-over) Doesn't he look peaceful.
>   FRED: (voice-over) Yeah, well. . . .
>   ELSIE: (v-o.) His colour ain't too good,
>   though.
>   FRED: (v-o.) Yeah, well. . . .
>   ELSIE: (v-o.) Still, it might not be for long.
>
>   DAD's eyes snap open. He stares straight
>   forward for a moment, then shoots his eyes from
>   side to side.

CAMERA pulls back to reveal ELSIE and
FRED standing on either side of the bed, in
reverent attitudes as one might adopt at a
graveside. FRED holds his cap across his chest.

> DAD: What do you mean, it might not be for
> long?
> ELSIE: Hallo, Dad.
> DAD: Hallo. What do you mean, it might not
> be for long?
> ELSIE: How you feeling, Dad?
> DAD: Fine! What do you mean, it might not
> be for long?
> ELSIE: He says he's feeling fine, Fred.
> FRED: Yeah, well. . ..
> DAD: What are you telling him for? Don't he
> understand English?
> ELSIE: He's my husband, Dad. He has a right
> to know.
> DAD: A right to know what?
> ELSIE: Well, that you say you're feeling fine,
> Dad.
> DAD: But I do feel fine.
> ELSIE: Well, then!
> FRED: Yeah, well, then.

We have now established the characters. We can
proceed with the despondency spreading.
DAD gives an exasperated sigh and glowers at them.

> DAD: What you doing here anyway? I thought
> this was your Bingo night.
> ELSIE: Oh, well, we just thought we'd come
> and cheer you up. While we had the chance.

41

FRED: And besides, the Bingo hall burnt down yesterday.

DAD: Chance? Chance? While you had the chance?

ELSIE: I don't know what you're on about. I don't. Honest. Unless. . . .

DAD: Unless? Unless what?

ELSIE: Unless nothing. It's just – well I don't suppose the doctor said anything when he was in just now.

DAD: Eh? No, he didn't. He just looked, and hummed a bit, and then he smiled, and walked away.

ELSIE: Yes. Well. He never tells you anything, that Doctor Phillips.

(to FRED)

You remember how he was with Mrs King?

FRED: Yeah. Mrs King.

ELSIE: Never told her a thing. Then, just a week later, Bang! Wallop! Just like that! The shock nearly carried poor Mr King off to his grave.

DAD: (alarmed) Mrs King? What happened to her?

ELSIE: She had twins. And that Doctor Phillips never said a word.

FRED: Ted King said plenty.

ELSIE: He was entitled. After all, he'd been at sea for a year.

The above "Mrs King" section is what I call a relevant diversion. It is the kind of insertion which is not only permissible but also welcome in the long sketch, whereas it would greatly interfere with the flow of anything shorter. There are two criteria. An insertion

42

should arise out of the main theme dialogue, and it should be funny.

> DAD: Well, I'm all right. Doctor Phillips didn't say nothing 'cos there was nothing to say. There ain't anything wrong with me.
> ELSIE: (heavily reassuring) No. Of course not, Dad.
> FRED: Yeah, well. . . .
> ELSIE: Don't, Fred. You'll only worry him.
> DAD: (glaring at FRED) He always has.

DAD picks up a magazine from his locker, opens it, rustles it loudly and makes a great show of becoming engrossed in it.

> DAD: Now, if you don't mind.
> ELSIE: No, of course not, Dad. You just go right ahead and read your nice magazine.

DAD grunts and disappears behind his magazine.

> FRED: Just don't start any serials, eh.

DAD drops the magazine and glares at FRED, who stares woodenly back. ELSIE hurriedly intervenes.

> ELSIE: That was just Fred's little joke, Dad.
> FRED: I got it out of one of them things you get at Christmas.
> ELSIE: Crackers.
> DAD: He always was.

DAD retires behind the magazine.

ELSIE and FRED face each other across the bed and engage in a conversation in which only their lips move and no sound comes out.

FRED: (mouth only) Ask him.

He jerks his head towards the reading figure.

ELSIE: (mouth only) Not now.

They ad-lib a silent conversation, which takes them to the foot of the bed, where FRED measures DAD's feet with hands held apart, and compares them with his own foot. They move back up to the head of the bed, still arguing silently.
DAD looks up from his magazine and follows the silent dialogue for a couple of speeches, his head turning from side to side like a spectator at Wimbledon. ELSIE becomes aware of DAD's interest. The mouthing ceases. She gazes down at him with a false smile.

ELSIE: Nice book, is it, Dad?
DAD: Never mind the book. You're hiding something from me, aren't you?
ELSIE: (exaggerated innocence) Whatever makes you think that, Dad?
DAD: You've been talking to the doctor.
ELSIE: What? Me? No! Never!
FRED: And anyway, what do doctors know about it?
ELSIE: That's right. You're always reading in the papers where a doctor says one thing and it turns out to be something else entirely.

44

FRED: Yeah.

ELSIE: There. So you see, if we had been speaking to Doctor Phillips, and we weren't speaking to Doctor Phillips, well, it doesn't mean it's as bad as he says.

DAD: What did he say? What did he say?

ELSIE: Eh? Well, let me see now. Funny, that. I can't seem to remember.

FRED: It was something about –

ELSIE: (hurriedly) And Fred can't seem to remember neither.

FRED: Yeah, well. . . .

There is a short pause while DAD looks from one to the other, wondering what is going on. ELSIE looks back at him reassuringly, FRED wooden-faced.

ELSIE: Believe me, Dad. There's nothing to worry about.

DAD starts to settle back and relax.

FRED: And besides, you'll never miss them.

DAD shoots upright again.

DAD: Miss them? Miss what? What did he say? What did that doctor say?

ELSIE: Steady on, Dad. You mustn't go upsetting yourself.

FRED: And you don't have much call for them at your age.

DAD: But . . . but . . . but. . . . That's rubbish. I'm still in my prime.

ELSIE: Oh, come off it, Dad. The last time

45

they were in action was ten years ago at your silver wedding.

DAD: How the hell do you know?

ELSIE: Mum told me. She said you'd only used them twice, and the first time they made your legs go all funny.

DAD: That's a downright lie!

ELSIE: And anyway, Fred needs them more than you do.

DAD: Fred? What does he want with them?

ELSIE: His own are worn out. And him and me are doing the cabaret at the church social on Saturday.

DAD: No! I'd rather die! And when I do he's not having them. I'll leave them to Medical Science.

ELSIE: Medical Science? What would Medical Science want with them?

DAD: (almost weeping) They can't take them away. They've got memories. And I only came in here for my ingrowing toe-nails.

ELSIE: Exactly.

DAD: If they touch anything else I'll sue. I've had them all my life and they'll go with me to the grave.

ELSIE: What are you talking about, Dad? Mum bought them for you in Marks & Spencers in 1974.

DAD's eyes widen with astonishment.

FRED: Don't worry. I'll look after them. I'll give them a good polish with a chamois leather every time I use them.

46

DAD's eyes roll up in his head. He falls back on the pillow in a faint.
FRED and ELSIE exchange worried glances across the bed.

> FRED: I didn't think he'd take it like that.
> ELSIE: After all, all we want is his old dancing pumps.

FADE.

To sum up the pseudo-realist approach, you take a normal, everyday, recognizable situation. This could be a hospital, as above, a stalled lift, a bus queue, a doctor's waiting room, almost any situation or circumstance in which a small group of people can meet, confront each other, and promote misunderstandings. All you have to do then is to create the characters, which, in your mind, will give you the elements of comedy that you need to make your point. It is also advisable, in the pseudo-realist approach, to have a point before you start writing. In other words, have a pay-off in mind. It does not have to be the exact punch-line, but you must know which effect you are aiming at. In the hospital sketch above, for instance, I knew at the start that the pay-off would have something to do with footwear as one side of the misunderstanding. It was only in writing the last couple of pages that dancing pumps presented themselves as the definitive answer.

In the zany approach the world is your oyster. Time and place are at the mercy of your ball-point or typing finger. Imagination is king.

If you have a funny idea set in a nudist colony on Mount Everest, write it. Julius Caesar landing in

Britain and having to go through customs? Great! Mr Spock retired and running a bicycle repair shop? Go ahead. Henry VIII and dating agency? Why not?

What we are going for here are laughs. There is one important rule in this field. You are probably going to establish an impossible or at least unlikely premise. Fine. But once that outrageous premise is established and accepted by your audience, everything that follows must obey the logic of the original idea.

Let us look for an idea.

Shakespeare has made a fair contribution to English literature. Why shouldn't he contribute to TV comedy. But was it Shakespeare or Francis Bacon? Why should we argue. Let's team them up, like Muir and Norden, or Galton and Simpson, and see what they can do for us.

FADE IN:
EXT. ELIZABETHAN-TYPE OFFICE
BLOCK. (Library still)
Sound F/X: Elizabethan music.
MIX TO:
OFFICE DOOR.
Stained glass panel on door bearing legend:
BACON & SHAKESPEARE
Bespoke Playwrights
&
Advertising Consultants
MIX TO:
INT. ELIZABETHAN WRITERS' OFFICE.
Tudor oak beams. Leaded windows. Heavy oak table covered with parchment scrolls, ancient books, quill pens, and inkwells.
SIR FRANCIS BACON (DANDY PERIOD

COSTUME) is gazing moodily out of the window.
WILL SHAKESPEARE (TATTY BLACK CLERICAL GARB) is seated at table, thinking deeply, nibbling a quill.

Already, visually we have established the pecking order.

Suddenly WILL snaps his fingers.

> WILL: I've got it, Frank.
> FRANK: Well, don't let me catch it.
> WILL: No, listen. You'll like this. It'll go right nice into *Richard III*. You know – that bit where he's sorting out his generals before the battle. Where is it, now.
> (leafs through manuscripts)
> Ah, here 'tis. You just have a harken to this, mate.
> (Declaims)
> York, Richmond, Gloucester,
> Get thee to friendly Hastings straight,
> And there disport thyselves in
> Pleasant revelry.
> Stout Bedford, you to fair
> Southampton hie –
> Warwick to Devon, Plymouth and the West.
> Surrey to Sussex, Essex unto Kent,
> Leicester to Norfolk, all on pleasure bent.
> Strength you will find to face our trials and sieges,
> After a week in sunny Bognor Regis.

He pauses and looks expectantly towards

FRANK for approval. FRANK looks stonily
back.

> FRANK: You're joking, of course.
> WILL: The Seaside Landladies Association
> will go a bundle on it. You'll see.
> FRANK: Stick to the accounts we've got.
> Have you done anything for the Tailor's Guild
> Export Drive to Scotland?
> WILL: Well, of course I did. Don't you
> remember? *Henry V* – at Agincourt.
> > (Declaims)
> "Once more into the breeks,
> dear friends, once more!"
> FRANK: Ah, yes. Good. Punchy. Why can't
> you turn out stuff like that every time?
> WILL: I could, but these stupid plays keep
> getting in the way.
> FRANK: (sighs) 'Tis sad that a talent such as
> mine should be associated with these sordid
> commercials.
> WILL: Now, you look here, mate. We're not
> in this for the good of literature, you know.
> We need the money. D'you know, when I came
> up to London first, all I earned was half a
> groat – for holding a horse. And I spent that
> on getting my shoes cleaned.
> FRANK: Rather extravagant, wasn't it?
> WILL: Highly necessary. I was holding the
> wrong end.

This is about as far as we can go with just our two
adversaries. It is time to introduce a new element, in
this case a client, someone of the period who might
have something to advertize.

SOUND F/X; Knock on door.
SIR WALTER RALEIGH enters.

RALEIGH: Good morrow, good sirs. Bacon
and Shakespeare, the advertising chaps?
FRANK: (with a sigh) Guilty.

WILL rises to his feet.

WILL: Why! It's Sir Walter Raleigh.
RALEIGH: You know me?
WILL: Recognized you right away from the
Queen's footprint on the back of your cloak.
FRANK: Enough of this idle chit-chat. What
can we do for you, Sir Walter?
RALEIGH: I want you to advertise this.

He takes a large potato out of his pouch and lays
it on the table. FRANK and WILL eye it
apprehensively.

WILL: You don't want to advertise that, mate.
You want to keep it quiet.
FRANK: What exactly is it?
RALEIGH: It's something I picked up in
America.
WILL: You don't want us, you want a doctor.
FRANK: Let me do the talking, Will.
                    (to RALEIGH)
What does it do?
WILL: Nothing. It just lies there.
FRANK: Haven't you got a sonnet or
something you could be getting on with, Will?
RALEIGH: Actually, it's jolly interesting.

The Indians eat it, you know.
WILL: The filthy swine!

FRANK picks up a parchment from the table
and hands it to WILL.

FRANK: Will, this balcony scene from Romeo
and Juliet. Cut out the dirty bits.

WILL takes the parchment, shrugs, sits at table
and starts checking. FRANK picks up the potato
and studies it.

FRANK: Well, now, Sir Walter. Suppose you
just fill me in on the details – attraction-wise.
RALEIGH: Eh! oh. Ah. Yes. Well, the
important points to note are, One, it's a sort
of food thing, and Two, I've got seven
shiploads of the damn things down in
Plymouth.
FRANK: I see. Yes. Well, that seems to be
straightforward enough. What do you think,
Will?

WILL is engrossed in his parchment. He gives a
dirty chuckle and crosses out a passage with his
quill.

WILL: Cor! Dear, dear. How we ever thought
we'd get away with that! Still, I can use it
down the pub tonight.
                    (looks up)
What's that, Frank?
FRANK: This. What do you think?
RALEIGH: The Queen is very hot on it.

WILL: So I've heard, but how does she feel about that thing?

RALEIGH: Her Majesty is jolly anxious for it to get the widest possible publicity.

FRANK: Oh, noble queen. Her only thought, to feed her starving people.

RALEIGH: Oh, absolutely. And she's got half-shares in my seven shiploads.

WILL has been eyeing the potato thoughtfully.

WILL: Has it got a name?

RALEIGH: Oh, goodness gracious, yes. The Indians call it aka-wanoo-tana-hini-widgey-wodgey-nooboo-flug. It means, little dirty brown eating stone with the soft fattening centre.

WILL: We'll never get that on the packet.

FRANK: We need something – ah – something – er –

WILL: Shorter.

FRANK: More switched on brevity-wise. Any ideas, Will?

WILL: I might have.

FRANK: Right. Let's lay it on the chopping block and see who takes a swing at it.

WILL: How about if we use bits of the Indian name?

FRANK: Like, such as?

WILL: Aka-flug. Widgey-wodgey, nooboo.

FRANK: Yes. I suppose one of them will have to do. But which one?

WILL: We'll count for it. You be aka-flug, Frank, Sir Walter will be widgey-wodgey, and I'll be nooboo. Right?

OTHER TWO: Right.

They each hold out their fists. WILL starts
counting.

> WILL: One potato, two potato, three potato,
> four. Five po. . . .

He breaks off, with a sudden idea.

> WILL: Wait a minute! That's it! We'll call it –
> potato!
> FRANK: Potato! But of course! What else?
> RALEIGH: I say, why potato?
> WILL: Because it looks like a potato.
> RALEIGH: (uncomprehending) Oh. Yes. Of
> course. What else?
> FRANK: (briskly) Right, now, Will. Which of
> our plays can take a potato commercial?

After a short pause for thought, WILL snaps his
fingers.

> WILL: Got it. Shove this up your doublet and
> see if it tickles. Picture it. *Macbeth*. That bit
> where the three witches are doing the big
> number round the cauldron. Right?

The other two listen eagerly and nod their heads.

> WILL: Round they go.
> >   (acts it out)
> Double, double, toil and trouble,
> Fire burn and cauldron bubble,
> Fillet of a fenny snake,

In the cauldron boil and bake.
Eye of newt and toe of frog,
Wool of bat and tongue of dog,
For a charm of powerful trouble,
Like a hell-broth boil and bubble. . . .

He pauses.

> BOTH: Yes? Yes?
> WILL: Then one of the girls chucks in a
> potato and the whole ruddy lot goes up.

It is round about here that we ought to be thinking ourselves towards a pay-off. With the potato as one of our central characters, the grave-digger scene from *Hamlet* seems to offer fertile soil. We should therefore start edging in that direction.

FRANK gives WILL a long hard look and shakes his head sadly.

> FRANK: You've been on the happy powders
> again, haven't you?
> WILL: (miffed) All right, Mr Clever. You have
> a go, then. See how you get on.

WILL sits down at the table and sulks. FRANK crosses to him and pats him on the shoulder.

> FRANK: Oh, come on, Will. Don't be like that.

WILL angrily shrugs him off. FRANK puts his hand back on WILL's shoulder.

> FRANK: We're a team, aren't we?
> WILL: Some team! I do all the work and you
> get all the credit.

FRANK: (cajoling) Will, old friend, old comrade, old soul-mate.

WILL turns his back on him. FRANK ponders, comes to a decision.

FRANK: Tell you what. I'll let you write *Hamlet*.
WILL: (brightening) *Hamlet*? *Hamlet*, Prince of Denmark?
FRANK: (resignedly) Yes. *Hamlet*, Prince of Denmark.
WILL: (suspiciously) Ah, but will you let me write To Be or Not To Be? . . . That is the question.
FRANK: Yes. You can put that in.
WILL: And the ghost? And the poison in the earhole? And the old geezer getting stabbed in the arras?
FRANK: And don't forget the potato.
WILL: I've got just the place for it. Right. Where's me quill and parchment?

He sits at the desk and starts scribbling, muttering to himself the while.

WILL: Hamlet Prince of Denmark. Act One, Scene One. The battlements at Elsinore. I can do me lot here. Murder, suicide, treason, insanity. . . .

He scribbles away furiously, growling and cackling mysteriously.
CUT TO:
TWO-SHOT: RALEIGH and FRANK.

RALEIGH: (anxiously) Is he – well – er – I mean – shouldn't we – ?

FRANK: (great show of confidence) Don't worry. It'll be all right on the night.

MIX TO:
PLAYBILL: GLOBE THEATRE
            HAMLET, PRINCE OF DENMARK
                        by
                WILL SHAKESPEARE
MIX TO:
STAGE OF GLOBE THEATRE.
GRAVEDIGGER SCENE SET.

HAMLET standing by open grave holding skull. WILL, as grave digger standing in grave with shovel.

HAMLET: Alas, poor Yorick! I knew him, Horatio. A fellow of infinite jest.
                (looks into grave)
Prithee, good oaf, what lies there at your feet?

WILL looks down, bends, stands up again holding a large potato.

WILL: Marry, kind sir, tis treasure from the Indies
That cleareth spots and cureth evil windies.
It bringeth shine to eyes and red to lips,
Let you but eat it boiled or fried as chips.
Banisheth aches and pains and such-like woes,
Charmeth unsightly warts and corns from toes.
And if you should want the wit of learned Plato,
Step up, step up, and get your hot potato.

He produces a tray of potatoes from the grave, hangs it round his neck and turns towards the audience.

SOUND F/X: Vast, disapproving audience noises.
WILL is deluged by a hail of potatoes.
FADE.

Just because this is a longer sketch than the one you tried in the last chapter it does not mean that you can relax discipline and take a more leisurely approach. You still have the obligation to make people laugh at least at the same frequency.

It does allow you, however, to widen your range of humour. You can go deeper into the characters that you create. You have the device of the "relevant diversion" to provide extra laughs.

In the pub/man/dog short sketch you are dealing basically with a recognizable joke or anecdote. Your dialogue will therefore be more or less confined to leading towards the pay-off. In the longer form you may find laughter in a discussion of how the dog gets on with the neighbours, or the man's wife, or the difficulties of feeding it, or whatever.

I cannot emphasize too strongly the importance of the dialogue in comedy sketches. It is vital that any dialogue provided should belong exclusively to the character for whom it was written. This seems so obvious a statement as to appear superfluous, but in my script editorial days I saw too many sketches where this simple rule was ignored.

When you start writing sketches examine carefully every line of dialogue you set down. Compare it with the characters you have established. Could it have been said by anyone else in the sketch? If so, does it matter?

In 99 cases out of 100 it will. With experience you will get a feel for your creations, and recognize instinctively if they are staying within their identities. Until then, be alert.

Chapter Six

SITUATIONS WANTED

Devise, wit! Write, pen!

Love's Labour's Lost

There may be those among you who will be quite content, indeed delighted, to break into television comedy writing at the sketch and quickie level, and to cultivate this particular field for the rest of your natural creative life.

This is an admirable ambition, and anyone who denigrates it should be treated with contumely, cool detachment, and a poke in the eye with a sharp typewriter.

The ultimate goal for many of you, however, will be the half-hour comedy format.

I have deliberately avoided the catch-all term "situation comedy", mainly because I find it confusing as a description.

All comedy is "situation". It is how a particular character or characters will behave in a given situation which generates comedy, and I can think of no half-hour comedy series in my time that did not depend for the major part of its success on the characters the writer created.

Take any of the classic comedy series, like "Steptoe and Son", by Galton and Simpson, for instance.

The situation was a father and son, trapped by circumstance in the same house, the same business.

These are the ingredients of tragedy, not comedy, until the characters unfold, but once father and son meet on the screen there is little for us to do but laugh till our sides ache.

The term "situation comedy" does gain a certain validity when it is applied to established comedians or comedy actors.

Here the public persona of an already popular performer is built upon, so situations must be created in which the traits and quirks of that figure can be exploited to the full.

In "The Blood Donor" episode of "Hancock's Half-Hour", once Tony Hancock enters the waiting room we know that laughter is inevitable, not because giving blood is particularly hilarious, but because we know that Hancock giving blood, under the guidance of Ray Galton and Alan Simpson, will supply us with entertainment of the highest order.

The same is true of Charlie Drake in "The Worker", a series on which I collaborated with Charlie for 25 episodes.

Charlie, in my view, was, at the height of his talents, one of the greatest clowns this country has ever seen. He was, in his prime, an intensely physical performer, relying rather more on comic business and movement than on mere words, though they had an important role.

Here the situation was of vital significance. We started off with the character and talents of Charlie, playing the part of a man whose only ambition was to get a job and keep it.

(This would not be a fun theme now, in the unemployed 80s, but in the swinging 60s it was valid).

In Charlie's case, however, every job he turned his hand to ended in disaster.

The format was simple. Each episode started off with Charlie visiting the labour exchange, (today the job centre), to explain to the long-suffering Mr Pugh (Henry Magee), how the last job had disintegrated into mayhem. After suitable recriminations Pugh would send Charlie out again on another doomed assignment.

That was the easy part. Now we had to create a situation in which Charlie could display his powers.

Real life situations were of little use in this context. They served as starting points, but we had to extend, extrapolate and expand, up to, and sometimes beyond, the limits of possibility, in order to let Charlie's capabilities have full rein.

Writing for Norman Wisdom on the other hand, allowed for closer adherence to reality, although there were strong clowning elements in his armoury, but there was still room for exaggeration under comic licence.

Nowadays, however, we do not seem to have the larger-than-life character comedians, like Hancock and Drake, Wisdom or Worth, comedians who were capable of donning the mantle of a half-hour story series without losing their own personalities.

We have plenty of excellent comedians, and therefore, theoretically, plenty of opportunities for the budding TV comedy writer who is prepared to work hard at learning the trade. We have stand-up comedians, like Jasper Carrott, who simply stand up and comede. We have sketch comedians like Russ Abbot, or Smith and Jones who leap blithely from one character and situation to another. We have Cannon and Ball, and Rory Bremner, who do both. And of course, and, until recently, we had the two Ronnies who do everything.

But there is no doubt that the comedy actor has taken over, certainly as far as the half-hour comedy series is concerned.

For the writer this has been a boon. Not only has it given writers access to a brilliant array of outstanding talents, but it has also broadened the scope and treatment of the subject matter that can be dealt with.

It has given the writer the chance to create true situation comedies, without the brief of having to tailor them to strong, recognizable and sacrosanct personalities. These true situation comedies are still few and far between. "Just Good Friends" comes to mind, in which a woman who had been left standing at the altar some years previously met up with the jilter, a real-life situation enchanced by the characters created by the writer and the performance of the actors involved.

Carla Lane's "The Mistress" also comes into this category. Again the situation, an eternal triangle, is the basic driving force, and again it is the brilliance of the writing and the excellence of the cast which make it work. Watch all the half-hour comedy series that come to your screen. Analyse them. See how many you think are true situation comedies and how many rely more on characters for their laughs.

Character comedy is a little more easy to recognize. In this format the "situation" is more often than not simply an environment. In "The Army Game", for instance, the situation was simply the Army. All the comedy came from the characters, from Sergeant-Majors Bullimore or Snudge, and their endless battles with the boys of hut 29. Look too, at the king of character comedy, Ronnie Barker. What does he need with a situation? All he seems to require is a shop, as in "Open All Hours", or a prison, as in "Porridge", plus, naturally, a script written by people who know their business.

The most common vehicle is of course the domestic comedy, or comedy based on family life. It was one of the earliest forms of comedy series and is still very much with us. Over the years TV has presented family comedy at almost every socio-economic level, from the working class roots of "The Larkins", the pickle factory of "Nearest and Dearest", or Carla Lane's "Bread"; through the middle-class meanderings of "Marriage Lines", "Terry and June", or "Mother Makes Three"; to the upper-crusty county set of "To the Manor Born".

It seems safe ground for a comedy writer to work on. After all, the vast majority of us have grown up in families, and in every family there are probably more moments of low comedy than high drama. How about that time Aunt Mabel got locked in the outside loo with the policeman? Or the day dad fixed the wireless set and blew every fuse in the neighbourhood? Or the time sister Anna got a whistle to deal with obscene phone-calls and deafened the vicar? Oh, yes, they were all uproarious at the time, but have you enough of them to pack a 30 minute slot every Tuesday night for 13 weeks?

Unless you grew up in a very weird family the answer is obviously, no. However, you do have something to build on, and you would have to have lived a very sheltered life indeed not to have picked up equally hilarious family incidents from your neighbourhood.

Fine. It is safe ground, because we all know about families and domestic crises, and if we do it right all the viewers will be able to relate to it. Domestic comedy is also the most common format, and highly popular with

SLEEPER: What about at night?

BULL turns and looks at him with a sneer.

BULL: Well! We do wake up sometime, then.
SLEEPER: I was thinking.
BULL: There's no need to strain yourself. I'm
the leader, I'll do the thinking round here,
thank you very much.
SLEEPER: So what about at night?
BULL: What do you mean, what about at
night?
SLEEPER: We often get fire at night. The sun
goes away at night. So where does the fire
come from at night?
BULL: Well, from the moon, of course.
Yeah. That's it. At night bits break off the
moon and fall down and hit the trees, and –
wallop! – we've got fire.
SLEEPER: But the moon isn't hot. It's cold.
BULL: Eh? Oh. Yes. Well. . . .
NOSE: He's got a point, there.
SLEEPER: And another thing. The bits that
break off the moon don't fall down. They fall
up.
BULL: What are you talking about?
SLEEPER: You look up at the sky at night
when there are no clouds about. You can see
all the little bits that have broken off the moon.
They're stuck on the black stuff above it, all
over the place.
BULL: Ah Yes. Well. . . .
NOSE: He's got another point, there.
BULL: You keep out of this.
                    (to SLEEPER)

And what makes you think all them little lights
in the sky at night are bits that have broken
off the moon?
SLEEPER: Well, for one thing, it keeps
getting smaller.
NOSE: He's got a. . . .
BULL: I won't tell you again.

(to SLEEPER)

All right, Know-All. Tell me this. What about
when the moon gets bigger?
SLEEPER: Oh, that's easy. That's when the
little bits fall back on to it.
BULL: (lost) You what?
SLEEPER: Look.

He picks up a stone, throws it up in the air and
catches it.

SLEEPER: When I throw this stone up in the
air it falls down again.
BULL: I see. So there's somebody up there on
the moon throwing little bits of it up into the
sky to make little lights, and then they all fall
back on him.
SLEEPER: Well, it's just an idea.
BULL: (pressing home the attack) And how
did this thrower of yours get up on to the moon
in the first place, eh?
SLEEPER: I haven't worked that out yet.
BULL: Oh, go back to sleep.
SLEEPER: And then again, the question
arises, if, as you say, bits keep breaking off
the sun to give us fire, why doesn't the sun get
smaller?

BULL: (grandly) I haven't worked that out yet.

There is a great crash of thunder almost overhead.

BULL: Right. Here we go. It'll soon be dinner-time.

They all gather expectantly round BULL, gazing eagerly out into the approaching storm.
There is another thunder clap, and a great flash of lightning.
CUT TO:
LIBRARY FILM. FOREST FIRE BEING STARTED BY FORK OF LIGHTNING.
CUT TO:
GROUP ON HILLSIDE.
They all start cheering like mad, except for BULL who looks smug.

BULL: I told you. Didn't I tell you?
(to NOSE)
Right, lad. Off you go.

NOSE drops the animal carcass and sets off down the hill at the gallop. The others watch him go, cheering him on. Smoke begins to drift up around them.

ALL: (ad-lib) Go on, Nose! Go on! Get closer! That one over there!

Their shouts of encouragement are punctuated

83

by distant cries of pain and anguish as NOSE encounters the flames.

    BULL: No. Not that one! A bigger one! Yes! That one over there!

There is another tremendous thunderclap just above them. A few large raindrops thud down on the hillside around them. A silence falls on the group. They look at each other aghast.

    BULL: Right! Everyone into the cave!

Everyone turns and scuttles off across the hillside, SLEEPER grabbing up the animal carcass as he goes. BULL stays a moment longer to shout instructions to NOSE.
CUT TO:
NOSE emerging from bank of smoke dragging a large tree branch, blazing merrily. NOSE himself is beginning to smoulder.
CUT TO:
HILLSIDE:

    BULL: Nose! The cave! Bring it to the cave!

The rain starts streaming. BULL turns and runs.
CUT TO:

6. INT. CAVE.
It is quite a large cave, with plenty of evidence of human habitation, piles of straw bedding, odd bones, etc.
The group begin to straggle in, rather damp and panting from their exertions. BULL arrives last,

and remains in the entrance, still yelling at
NOSE.

   BULL: Faster! Faster! Put some effort into it,
   you useless gorilla!

NOSE finally staggers into the cave with the thick
end of the tree still on his shoulders. He is
soaked to the skin, grimy, with little wisps of
smoke and steam rising from various parts of his
body.
The tree is even wetter. A tiny flame still putters
at the end of one of the branches. As the group
gathers round, the tree gives up it's seed of
warmth in a ghostly hiss. The tribe stands
around it, like mourners at a funeral. The silence
is finally broken by OLD COW.

   OLD COW: I suppose this means another five-
   day wait for our dinner.
   BULL: Why don't we just eat it as it is?

FADE.

   Right. Let's pause for a moment and examine what
we have got so far.
   The first thing we notice is that we have a rather
lengthy opening scene for our pilot script.
   Why is it rather lengthy?
   Because I, the writer, decided that that was required.
   Why did I think that an opening scene of this length
was required?
   Because my subject-matter dictated it.
   I am dealing with a group of people, a tribe, in
which there are six main characters essential to the
development of my theme. The sooner I introduce my

85

audience to them, the sooner I can get on with my story. I must also lay down the foundations of theme and story as early as possible. This may take a little time.

In a normal domestic comedy, I might have opened in a living room, with father and/or mother, who would talk a little, revealing something of their relationship with each other, and their attitudes to family, work, life, likes and dislikes. In the time I spent on my hillside, the normal domestic comedy might have moved to father's office; the kitchen; the back of a taxi; a supermarket checkout; the local Job Centre. It would have introduced at suitable moments the kids, father's business partner and/or secretary, aunt Mabel, or whoever was going to become involved throughout the series.

If you decide that this is what you require for your pilot script, great! No argument! Just make sure you get as much into your fast, snappy opening scenes as I got into my hillside.

1. Establish your characters.
2. Establish their environment.
3. Establish their place in that environment.
4. Establish the pecking order.
5. Establish relationships. Who sides with whom. Who is against whom. Who are the troublemakers either intentionally or merely accident prone.
6. Don't forget it is a comedy.
7. Start your story.

Check this list against my opening scene. I think you will find they are all adequately covered.

The length of the scene might worry you. Look at it another way. It may seem one long scene, but it is actually a number of scenes within a scene. In the hands of an intelligent director you would hardly notice otherwise.

So now we are up and running. The characters are loaded, our story has started, (viz. our episode title "Fire!" and the constant harping on it in our opening scene) so let us see what happens next.

7 INT. CAVE. DAY.
OLD COW and COW are squatting on the cave floor plucking the hairs off the animal carcass one by one. FLOWER is sulking in a corner. SLEEPER is in his usual meditative position against a wall. NOSE is at the cave mouth gazing out at the storm. BULL is pacing up and down in surly mood.
BULL strides over to COW and OLD COW and glares down at them.

BULL: Ain't you got that dinner ready yet?
OLD COW: Don't blame us. You're the one that likes your food fancied up.
BULL: (defensively) Well! The hairs stick in my teeth.
OLD COW: They don't stick in mine.

She grins a huge toothless grin. BULL grimaces at the sight and turns away.

BULL: Just get on with it.
OLD COW: If you'd got us fire like you said we'd be all right, wouldn't we. We'd have all the hair burnt off by now.
COW: She's right, you know.
BULL: Do you want a smile like hers?

OLD COW: It's all you're good for, isn't it, punching folks in the mouth?
BULL: Another word and there'll be one less for dinner.
OLD COW: Yeah, that's right. Shout at a poor old woman. That's all you can do.
BULL: I'll show you what I can do.
OLD COW: We've seen what you can do. Nothing.

BULL gives a mighty roar, raises his club and takes a mighty swing at her. She ducks back. He misses. The club shatters against the cave wall. He looks at the little stump left in his hand, roars again and throws it at her. She retreats further into the cave. BULL follows. The rest of the tribe form a small crowd of interested spectators and drift after them.
CUT TO:
REAR OF CAVE.
OLD COW backs in, followed by BULL, and the others. BULL is picking chunks of rock from the floor and hurling them at her. Shrieking, OLD COW retreats to the back wall of the cave and huddles against it. BULL hurls on.
A rock thuds into the wall beside OLD COW. It breaks off a flake of stone, revealing a dull metallic gleam. Just below it is a pile of old straw bedding.
BULL bends down and picks up another stone. Unknown to him it is a flint. He throws it at her. It misses her and strikes the metallic gleam. A spark leaps out and falls on the straw below.
BULL keeps throwing stones at OLD COW. She goes on shrieking and trying to avoid them.

Suddenly NOSE grabs BULL's arm and points.

NOSE: Bull! Look.

Everyone looks where he is pointing. A wisp of
smoke rises from the straw bedding. It bursts
into flame. Everyone watches with fascination.
Everyone but BULL.
He walks across to the fire and stamps it out.
There is a stunned silence. It is finally broken by
NOSE.

NOSE: Hem! Wasn't that fire?
BULL: Eh? Where?
NOSE: That thing. On the floor. Just now.
That you stood on.
BULL: Don't be stupid. Of course it wasn't.
SLEEPER: It looked like fire.
OLD COW: Felt like it, too. It got all hot up
my legs.
BULL: How could it have been fire? We've
got half a mountain above our heads. Any fire
dropping out of the sky couldn't possibly have
got down this far.
SLEEPER: Maybe it didn't drop out of the sky.
BULL: (amused incredulity) Didn't drop out
of the sky? Didn't drop out of the sky? Where
did it come from? Eh? I suppose it just jumped
out of the flaming wall!
SLEEPER: Well, as a matter of fact. . . .
BULL: (with a sigh) I dunno. You don't get
any better, do you?
SLEEPER: Well, actually –
BULL: Look, who is the fire expert round
here?

SLEEPER: Well, you are, but –
BULL: Now. Have I ever got you fire from
anywhere else, but up in them big, black,
rumbly clouds?
SLEEPER: Well, no, but –
BULL: Right, then. Shut up!
SLEEPER: But, Bull, what we just saw –

BULL grabs SLEEPER by the front of his fur
garment and hauls him up for an eyeball-to-
eyeball.

BULL: You're dabbling again, aren't you?
SLEEPER: No, Bull. Honest. I was just –
BULL: Oh, yes you are. You are dabbling in
the unnatural. You're always at it. Always
trying to change the world. Why can't you
leave well enough alone?
SLEEPER: Well, it's just – I keep getting these
sort of pictures in my head, like – well – like
it might make life a bit easier.
BULL: But they don't make life any easier,
do they, these head pictures? I mean, look at
that last idea of yours. When you tried to
make friends with a water buffalo.
SLEEPER: That was a good idea. If I could
have talked that water buffalo into joining this
tribe we would have had a regular supply of
meat everywhere we went.
BULL: It didn't work, though, did it? You
walk up to him, you start talking, and he chases
us all round the valley.
SLEEPER: Maybe it was something I said.

BULL gives up. He looks round for someone

else on whom to vent his spleen. COW is still plucking the carcass.

> BULL: Oi! Ain't that dinner ready yet?
> COW: No, and it won't be ready today if you keep interrupting.

BULL sighs, long-suffering. NOSE and FLOWER are sitting side by side with their backs to the cave wall. He strides over to them.

> BULL: Right. You. Let's go berry-picking.
> NOSE: (startled) Who? Me?
> BULL: Don't be filthy!

He grabs FLOWER by the wrist and pulls her upright and off towards the entrance to the cave. FLOWER goes reluctantly.

> FLOWER: Really! You and your berry-picking! It's all you ever think of, isn't it. Berry-picking mad, that's what you are.

They exit.
SLEEPER makes sure BULL has gone, then crosses to the site of the fire. The evidence is there in a little pile of ash. He examines it closely. He is joined by NOSE and OLD COW.

> NOSE: It was fire, wasn't it.
> OLD COW: Of course it was. Look! It burned my bottom.

(NOTE: You are now about to see man's first scientific research Programme begin.)

SLEEPER ponders deeply.

> SLEEPER: Bring us some of those dried
> leaves.

NOSE fetches them. SLEEPER piles them on
the little heap of ashes. They all sit back and
wait expectantly. Nothing happens.

> SLEEPER: Hmmm. I think there's something
> more to it. Now, what exactly was happening
> just before?
> NOSE: Bull threw a stone.
> SLEEPER: Right. Throw a stone.

NOSE picks up a stone and lobs it onto the pile
of leaves. They wait. Nothing.

> NOSE: Oh, well. It was just a shot in the dark.

He rises, ready to quit. SLEEPER stops him.

> SLEEPER: No. Hang on. That's not right.
> Bull was further away. Over there
> somewhere.

NOSE moves away to the approximate position.

> NOSE: About here?

SLEEPER examines the position critically,
makes minor adjustments.

> SLEEPER: Over a bit. A bit more. No. The
> other way. Back a bit. A bit more. Right.
> That's about it.

NOSE picks up a handful of stones and starts throwing them at the wall. Nothing.
NOSE shrugs.

>NOSE: Oh, well. Back to the flaming forest.
>SLEEPER: Not yet. Not yet. That wasn't the way it was. Not exactly. We've got to do it exactly the way it was. There is something missing.
>NOSE: Yeah. Old Cow.
>SLEEPER: (snaps fingers) Right! Old Cow!

OLD COW shuffles over to him. He places her against the wall. He turns to NOSE.

>SLEEPER: About there, would you say?
>NOSE: Yeah, well, just about. But she was jumping up and down.
>SLEEPER: (to OLD COW) Jump up and down.
>NOSE: And she was hollering.
>SLEEPER: (to OLD COW) And holler.

OLD COW looks at him bewildered.

>OLD COW: You what?
>SLEEPER: Jump up and down and holler.
>OLD COW: What for?
>SLEEPER: We're trying to make fire.
>OLD COW: You're not going to burn my bottom again.
>SLEEPER: No, of course not. We just want a little fire, that's all.
>OLD COW: Oh, all right. But you be careful, d'you hear?

SLEEPER: We'll be careful.

He crosses to NOSE, lines him up. Finally taps him on the shoulder.

SLEEPER: Right. Fire!

NOSE starts throwing stones. OLD COW ducks and dodges, shrieking the while as she did for BULL's onslaught. SLEEPER watches intently. One of the stones is a large flint. It hits the wall, unfortunately not in the right place and shatters.
CUT TO:
COW, SITTING TO ONE SIDE,
Shards of flint land on the floor beside her. She picks up a long sliver and examines it curiously.
CUT TO:
BACK WALL OF CAVE.
NOSE gets to the end of his ammunition. Still nothing.

SLEEPER: It's still not right, somehow.
NOSE: The only thing I can think of, Bull was shouting a bit, too.
SLEEPER: (nodding sagely) Good point. Right. Carry on.

NOSE picks up more stones and carries on throwing.

NOSE: Yah! Silly old cow! Rotten old hag! Gumsy old trotter. Yah!

Behind them BULL and FLOWER enter the cave, BULL looking surly, FLOWER pouting. BULL takes in the scene and storms forward.

94

BULL: What the bleeding thump is going on here?

SLEEPER turns round guiltily, forces a sheepish smile.

SLEEPER: Oh. Hallo, Bull. Didn't expect you back so soon. Pick any good berries?
FLOWER: I wouldn't let him. The ground was too wet.
BULL: Never mind the berries. You're at it again, aren't you?
SLEEPER: Eh? Who? Me? Oh, no. I was just –
BULL: Don't you "I was just" me. You were at it. you were dabbling in unnatural powers what you know not of. You're a bleeding menace, you are. What are you trying to do? Destroy the human race?
SLEEPER: Well, I just thought –
BULL: You thought? Who told you to think?
SLEEPER: Well, I –
BULL: If you think I'm going to stand here and let you think you've got another think coming.
SLEEPER: All I did was –

With a roar BULL grabs him by the fur coat and raises a hand to strike. COW intervenes.

COW: Now, just calm down, everybody. Dinner's nearly ready.

BULL glances round at her. His eyes widen in horror at what he sees.

COW is scraping the last of the hair off the
carcass with the long sliver of flint.
BULL strides across and snatches it out of her
hand.

   BULL: What the. . . !
   COW: Makes a lovely job of it. See?
   BULL: Where did you get this?
   COW: I saw it lying on the ground and I just
picked it up and I thought –
   BULL: You thought!
     (he shakes fist furiously at SLEEPER)
See? You've got her doing it now.
   COW: Give us it, Bull. It makes things so
much easier.
   BULL: If you'd been meant to do it that way
you'd have had these instead of fingers.
   COW: Oh, please, Bull.
   BULL: Never! If I was to let you go on using a
thing like this it could mean the end of
civilization as we know it.

He turns and hurls the sliver at the back wall of
the cave. It hits the metallic gleam near where
OLD COW is now squatting.
BULL paces up and down the cave haranguing
his people.

   BULL: I don't know why I bother with you
lot. Straight I don't. Here I am, working my
head to the bone to keep you in the style of
living which I've got you accustomed to, and
what thanks do I get? Eh? None. Not so much
as a nod, or a wink or a kiss my elbow. New!
Give us something new! That's all you lot ever

think of. But there ain't nothing new. I've been all round the world. I know. I've been to every corner of the earth that you can see from this cave-mouth, and it's the same all over. You start trying to change it and something terrible will happen. Like, it will tip over and we'll all fall off.

There is a scream from OLD COW. She has leapt to her feet and is slapping furiously at her garment which is smouldering, from the fire which is now burning merrily in the straw below the metallic gleam.

    SLEEPER: Quick! The food! Get the food on to it.

COW starts to drag the carcass towards the fire. Before she can reach it, BULL gets there first and stamps it out.
Everyone looks aghast.

    NOSE: What did you do that for?
    BULL: We can't put our food on that. We don't know where it's been!

He stands with his back to the cave wall, glaring at them. To his astonishment he finds them glaring back. They look as if they are about to mutiny.

    BULL: (a little less certainly) Well, I mean, it's not our kind of fire, is it? We get our fire from. . . .

The group are slowly closing in on him, menacingly. He is saved by a loud clap of thunder. He seizes on it.

    BULL: Hear that? You want fire? I'll get you fire.

He grabs up the large tree branch that NOSE had brought in earlier, and dashes out of the cave. There is a deafening peal of thunder and a blinding zigzag of lightning flashes across the cave mouth.
In a moment BULL comes staggering back into the cave, blackened and smouldering, smoke rising from his hair and furs, but with the tree branch burning.

    BULL: There's your fire. Honest. I don't know what you lot would do without me.

He sinks to the floor, unconscious.
ROLL END CAPTIONS.

So, now we have a pilot script which, if nothing else, will at least let a producer know how we handle story construction, dialogue, and comedy business. Let's assume he is impressed. I know I am.

His next question will be, "Funny piece, yes. But is there enough for a series?"

To convince him that there is, you should accompany your pilot script with some ideas on how the series will progress. As:

SERIES DEVELOPMENT.
As we have seen in the pilot script, man's first

98

attempts to master fire have proved abortive in the face of conservative tradition and brute-force authority. This search for fire will be a running theme throughout the series.

As the series progresses NOSE will question, and SLEEPER will theorize. BULL will contest SLEEPER's theories which always contain a sliver of logic. Time and again he is on the verge of a breakthrough that could advance humanity 1000 years, but a combination of BULL's attitudes and his own lack of solid knowledge turn the "Giant Step Forward" into a painful stumble.

Each episode will deal with one central thread of the development of civilization.

Example: The arts.

Muddy hands leave prints, the beginnings of cave-painting; Wet clay stepped on and kicked angrily into the fire, overnight crockery; SLEEPER notices the different pitches of voices and the various sounds made by hitting things and very nearly discovers music. A thin branch with a creeper attached to one end is causing a lot of trouble in the hands of NOSE. It keeps tripping people up and getting caught in things. SLEEPER manages to secure the creeper, which is shorter than the branch, to its other end. He finds that when he hits it with a stick it makes a pleasant twang. The stick gets entangled in the creeper. Trying to pull it out, the stick shoots across the clearing and nearly hits BULL. BULL immediately sees its possibility as a weapon, and music has to wait for another inventor.

Example: Matrimony.
NOSE poses a simple question. "Why does
BULL get all the crumpet?" Once a question
like that is asked the young men of the tribe will
never be the same. BULL realizes he must give
a little. His solution is to offer to his young hot-
bloods the services of OLD COW. COW and
FLOWER are more than a little interested in
helping the young men out. BULL has his hands
full preserving the status quo.

Other episodes will deal with themes like religion,
democracy, agriculture, natural science in general, all
discussed and determined at the level of the earliest
threshold of human intelligence.

WARNING!
It is important that the episodes be played for real.
Anachronisms are anathema. These are real people
with real problems, many of which, despite our
superior intelligence, we have not solved satisfactorily
to this day.

And there you have it. You have had your great idea
for a series. You have laid out the concept. You have
written your pilot script, you have indicated how the
series will develop. All you need now is luck.

The question may be crossing your mind: "If this
series presentation that he has put together is any good,
why hasn't he sent it in himself?"

The answer is simple.

I have.

And received the reply, in writing, from one of the
top TV companies that I warned you about at the
beginning of this chapter:

"Thank you for your suggested series 'We're Only Human', which we found most interesting and amusing. Unfortunately we have never produced anything in this vein, and can therefore make no acceptable assessment as to its possible audience impact. Yours sincerely. . . ."

Another of the top TV companies turned it down (again I have the letter) on the grounds that it was ahead of its time.

Yet another was more succinct. They simply said: "No thanks. We've already done 'The Flintstones'."

Good luck!

Chapter Seven

ALTERNATIVE(?) COMEDY

You beat your pate and fancy wit will come.

Anon.

I pondered long over the title to this chapter. I started off with the title "Alternative Comedy". I wondered what it meant. I tried "Alternative Comedy?". It seemed a little more significant. It implied that the comedy was in question.

When the phrase "Alternative Comedy" first started being bandied about in the late 70s, my original impression was indeed that comedy was in question. It appeared to consist entirely of people shouting at each other or at the world in general, with a built-in licence to offend. I found myself approaching the phrase semantically. There was comedy, which made you laugh, and there was alternative comedy, which didn't.

Still, it has its followers, and though it isn't my bag of nuts, who am I to condemn it.

I prefer to think of alternative comedy simply as covering the different fields of comedy, rather than the styles.

There is the television of the absurd, for instance. Two outstanding examples are "Monty Python's Flying Circus", and Spike Milligan's "Q5". "Monty Python" has become a classic. "Q5" is virtually forgotten. Why?

Both were the products of brilliant minds. Both had the same producer, Ian MacNaughton. What went wrong?

The key lies in one word, discipline, a vital element in writing for TV.

Spike, possibly the sharpest comic brain I have ever encountered, broadcast his comic creations like the biblical sower of seeds. In the "Goon Show" they landed in the imagination, where the listener could nurture them until they grew into wonderful mental landscapes. In television, however some fell by the wayside, and some on stony ground, because they were Spike's mental landscapes, and there were not enough people with Spike's imagination to go round.

The "Python" team started out the same way. In their first few shows they hurled weird concepts at the screen like buckshot. Some of them were bound to hit, but a lot of them missed. But from those early shows they learned what worked and what didn't, and in a very short time they were hitting just about everything.

In other words, they were learning their craft. They had accepted the discipline of the medium, and, though it may seem to be a strange word when applied to "Monty Python", they were exercising professional control. You just cannot communicate without it.

So far in this book we have looked at quickies, sketches (short and long) and the half-hour comedy format.

Let us look at some of the other alternatives (in the dictionary sense).

In the 60s the "Frost Report", but more significantly its illustrious offspring "That Was The Week That Was", brought satire to our screens. Nowadays we have "Spitting Image". In the old days we thought TWTWTW was hard-hitting and wicked. Compared to "Spitting Image" it was mere shadow-boxing.

If you think that "Spitting Image" is the target for your writing, consider it very carefully. Anarchistic though it may appear from your easy chair, it has its own rule-book, the discipline and control I keep harping on. Study the programme carefully, learn the rules. Stick to them.

Music must not be ignored as an instrument of comedy.

There are the hilarious musical medleys as performed by the two Ronnies, where they choose a theme, marching bands, barn dance, a ladies' choir, and put together a sequence of parodies of well-known songs pertinent to the setting. Alas! the two Ronnies are no longer in harness, and I fear it will be some considerable time before anyone else dares to emulate them, so there doesn't seem to be an immediate market there.

The song parody is still a valid device, however, so if you see a performer who uses it, and you have that kind of talent in your locker, why not have a go.

Another thing you can do with music is to set comedy action to a song. A simple example would be to take a song like "Tell Me Pretty Maiden," and set it perhaps in a park, with a soldier singing it to a nanny, with a baby in a pram between them, the baby interrupting the flow of romance by doing all the various things a baby can do.

Parody can also be applied to other things apart from music. Think of all the sketches you have seen which are parodies of well-known TV programmes, "This is Your Life", "Mastermind", quiz shows, all are fair game, and perhaps the fairest game of all is the TV commercial.

But whatever form of TV comedy you decide to write, approach it with caution, dedication, and a profound determination to communicate with the widest possible audience.

After all, writing comedy for television is a very serious business.

Chapter Eight

PRESENTATION

Neat, not gaudy. . . .

Charles Lamb

Over the years, I have been approached by many worthy citizens who aspire to writing for television. The usual introductory remark is, "I have this great idea for a television series. Why don't you write it up and we'll split the proceeds?"

Leaving aside the fact that none of these "Great Ideas" has ever appealed to me, my invariable answer, and I think the proper one, is, "Why don't you write it yourself?"

The first reaction to this is usually, "Oh, I wouldn't know how to go about it." Occasionally, however, the aspirant is a little more self-confident and wants to know how to set out his stall to the best advantage, what form it should take on the printed page.

Sometimes the request is for an old script, so that he can see exactly what a script looks like. If I provided an old rehearsal script it would look something like this:

AFTER OPENING CAPTIONS:
FADE IN:
1. INT. DOG AND DUCK. NIGHT.

ARNOLD AND ETHEL ARE SITTING AT A
CORNER TABLE. ETHEL IS BROODING
OVER A GIN AND TONIC WHILE ARNOLD
TRIES TO EAT HEDGEHOG-
FLAVOURED CRISPS WITH STUDIED
NONCHALANCE.

> ETHEL: Is that all you've got to say, then?
> ARNOLD: Yus.
> ETHEL: Not so much as a "Beg your Pardon"?
> ARNOLD: No.
> ETHEL: Right, then.
> ARNOLD: Right, then.

ETHEL TOSSES BACK HER DRINK,
STARTS TO COLLECT HER HANDBAG
ETC.

> ARNOLD: You going, then?
> ETHEL: (STANDING UP) I'm not staying.
> ARNOLD: (ASTONISHED) What you doing
> that for, then?
> ETHEL: You don't love me any more.
> ARNOLD: Of course I love you any more.

And so on and so on for anything up to 40-odd pages.

If you insist on using this format you will tend to double your stationery bill.

In earlier chapters I have used slightly different layouts. They are perfectly acceptable. The important thing is to make your meaning clear.

Remember the story-board concept. Lay out your sequence of word pictures unambiguously, comprehensibly, succinctly.

Be neat. Be clean. It is going to happen to you that

scripts are returned, and that you will, if you have any faith in them, try again at a different door. In time, depending on your self-belief, your scripts will become tattered and dog-eared. Make fresh copies. No producer should ever suspect that he is not the first to be honoured with your little gem.

This is where the word processor comes in handy. You can store sketches and scripts till required, then, when a new possible outlet appears, it is the work of a moment to change the names, add anything which might suit the latest market, run off a print and await results.

Chapter Nine

"WHO WILL BUY?"

The difficulty in life is choice.

George Moore.

So you have done it.

You have sat for countless hours in front of your television screens. You have watched all the comedy programmes with keen analytical eye. You have studied the techniques and effects that can be created. You know the capabilities of the performers – and their limitations. Gloriously funny ideas have formed in your mind and burgeoned into quickies, sketches, or series ideas. You have pounded away at your typewriter, or gazed greenfaced into the VDU of your word processor till the dead of night, and there, finally, before your very eyes, lies a sheet of paper with a quickie on it, or perhaps a sheaf of papers with the definitive half-hour comedy series.

What do you do next?

In the case of quickies and sketches, you want to catch the eye and ear of the producer of your target programme. His name will be plain and clear in the end captions, with a whole screen all to himself. Take a note of his name. Make sure you spell it correctly. (On such small details success or failure can hang.) Take note also of the company he works for. The addresses of all the companies can be found in the *Writers' and Artists' Yearbook* which is available in nearly all local libraries.

You will have to bear in mind that the programme you have just seen was probably recorded weeks or even months ago, and that the producer may well have moved on to pastures new. Send it to him anyway. If his forte is light entertainment sketch shows he will be doing more, and will therefore always be on the lookout for new and good material.

Send it to him, enclosing a stamped addressed envelope for its safe return. (There is a school of thought that sees this as a pre-admission of failure. It suggests, according to this theory, that you are already expecting your work to be returned. I disagree. It is first an act of courtesy, which is more likely to be appreciated. And second, there is more chance of getting your script back to try again in a more appreciative quarter.)

Don't be put off by rejection. If you believe that your material is good, keep trying. Somewhere out there there must be a producer with taste, who will recognize talent when he sees it.

If it is a series you are trying to sell the approach is rather different.

All the major TV companies have script departments whose function it is to find material for the screen. Again the *Yearbook* will supply the appropriate addresses.

You might also have a try at the head of light entertainment of a company. And, of course, should you land the big one they will have the added kudos of being able to claim that they discovered you.

There are now a growing number of independent producers and companies on the scene. It is worth keeping an eye open for their names at the end of a programme. These companies tend to come and go, so be careful how you set about contacting them. The *Yearbook* and a simple telephone call will soon reveal whether they are still in existence or not.

Where do agents fit in to the life of the new TV writer?

The answer is of course that they don't.

When you start out you are on your own. No agent will be prepared to give you the time of day. Once you begin to achieve, however, the sky will start to darken with their outstretched wings and eager beaks as they scent another meal ticket. There are good agents. Somewhere. Should the need arise, I pray you find one.

As soon as you can, you should join the Writers' Guild of Great Britain. It is not compulsory, but the further you go in this business, the more you will find it useful to have a sound organization behind you.

And there you have it. Perhaps the next time you yell at a TV screen "I could write better rubbish than that!" you'll be able to prove it.